THE
ROYAL
BALLET
TODAY

Published by THE WORLD PUBLISHING COMPANY
119 West 57th Street, New York 10019

Library of Congress Catalog Card No. 69-14463

First American Edition April 1969
First published in Great Britain 1968
by GEORGE G. HARRAP & CO. LTD.

© Keith Money 1968

All rights reserved. No part of this book may be
reproduced in any form without written permission
from the publishers, except for brief passages
included in a review appearing in a newspaper or
magazine.

BOOK DESIGNED BY KEITH MONEY

*Photographic printing
by Karl Ritter*

*Composed in Bembo and printed by
D. H. Greaves, Ltd., Scarborough*

The ROYAL BALLET TODAY

seen by KEITH MONEY

THE WORLD PUBLISHING COMPANY
NEW YORK CLEVELAND

PRINTED IN ENGLAND

NO OTHER ballet company in the world presents its audiences with such astonishingly varied programmes as does Britain's Royal Ballet. Its extensive resources, artistic and administrative, imbue it with the prestige and power necessary in its unique rôle as a treasure-house of the world's great ballets. A living reference museum, it can provide from its repertory a crammer course in one hundred years of choreographic evolution. The Royal Ballet's classical traditions have enabled it to preserve —albeit sometimes tenuously, the original forms of the grand Russian masterpieces of Petipa and Ivanov, as well as those by Fokine, Nijinska, Massine and the young Balanchine from Diaghilev's era.

Under its present director Sir Frederick Ashton, whose own choreographic masterpieces have increased our dance heritage, the company has continued this eclectic policy; to the work of its own protegées MacMillan and Cranko has been added—at last—a new masterwork by that expatriate prophet Antony Tudor, along with valuable Russian re-creations by the former Kirov dancer Rudolf Nureyev. The latter has also proved an awesome challenge to those emerging dancers who would strive to emulate him in the classroom, and on stage a unique foil to our greatest ballerina.

A host of superb leading dancers, backed by a superb *corps-de-ballet,* constantly being extended in an ever widening range of expressiveness—the combination is irresistible. No book can encompass really adequately such diverse riches, but I hope this volume will provide a fresh reminder of much that the Royal Ballet is doing today.

Roland Petit's
Paradise Lost

A theatrical grenade in an otherwise quiet season, Petit's mildly controversial creation was in no danger of being mistaken as a child of Milton once the curtain had risen on the neon count-down of Adam's birth. Pop imagery and P.V.C. replaced the celluloid chic of the Thirties without entirely removing hints of that era from the regimented ensemble movements. But the double work for the two principals was the pivotal core of the ballet, and Adam and Eve's first encounters with each other produced an involved and difficult 'calligraphy', tracing character-like images of strange beauty.

    The magnetic brilliance of the two leading dancers found full range; the ballet provided Nureyev with magnificent opportunities for employing that rare and idiomatic body plastique and stage persona, and allowed Fonteyn to reveal an effortless mastery as well as dazzling allure in yet another facet of her apparently inexhaustible range. The ballet is unlikely to survive in the permanent repertory without its original protagonists, yet a case could be made for the preservation of the extended pas de deux of the first section, containing as it does some compelling modern dance imagery.

RIGHT Margot Fonteyn and Rudolf Nureyev

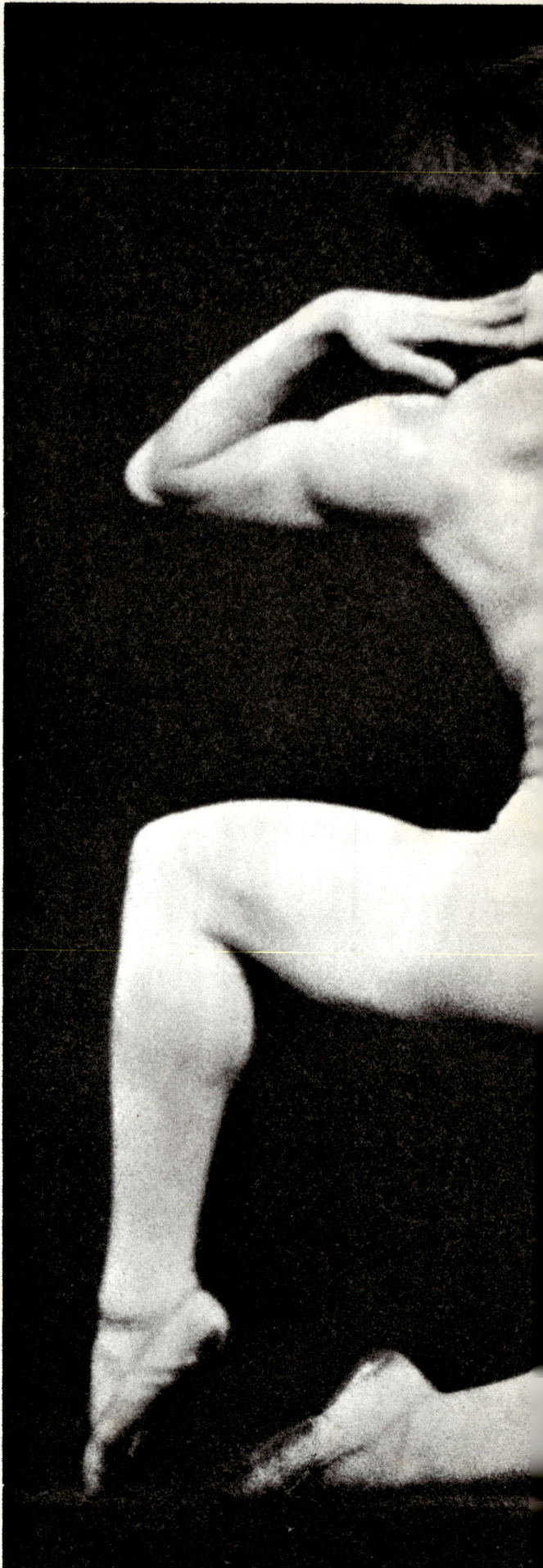

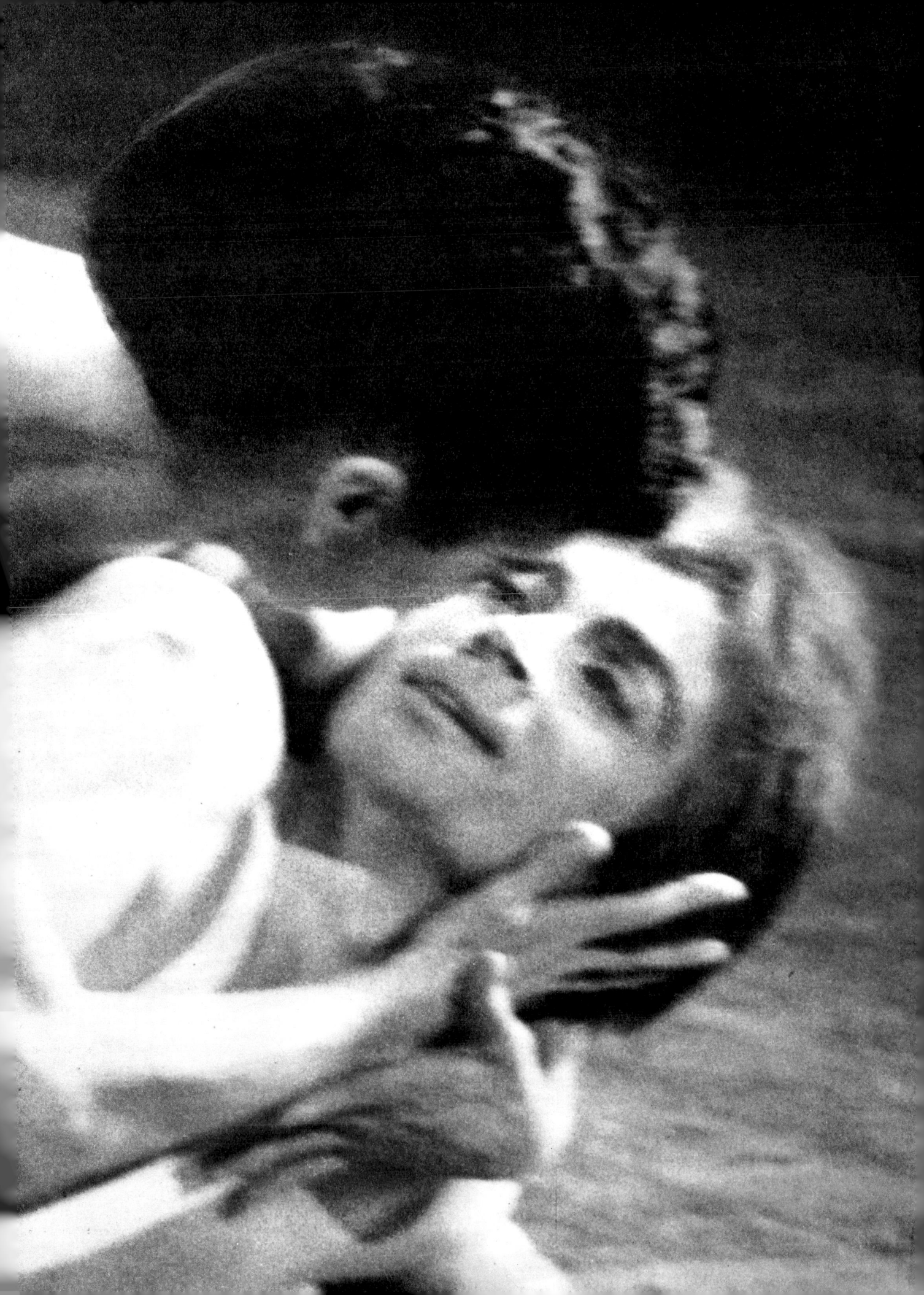

The Fall—
and Eve remains,
pondering sphinx-like
with the electrocuted
body of Adam

The final pieta-like tableau was
fortuitously arrived at—as is so
often the case in choreographic
creation. During a rehearsal
Fonteyn had to improvise to replace
an unmanageable exit with the
heavy 'corpse'. The solution gave
to the ballet an unexpectedly
profound conclusion

Bronislava Nijinska surrounded by soloists from the revival of her ballet. L. TO R. Robert Mead, Svetlana Beriosova, David Blair, Keith Rosson and Georgina Parkinson

Bronislava Nijinska's
Les Biches

Frederick Ashton has long expressed his indebtedness to the early inspiration he gained from Nijinska's works, in particular the slightly enigmatic *Les Biches,* with its transmuted classical idiom and sly humour trapping the frivolity of an era with devastating accuracy. Not surprisingly, *Les Biches* was the first of two Nijinska works which the Royal Ballet's Director asked the choreographer to revive for his company. Nijinska was in her element; adoring and adored, she had the dancers slaving for her unreservedly. The results, both in *Les Biches* and the very different *Les Noces* which followed, repaid all the effort. In *Les Biches,* the Riviera's pastel-coloured imagery seemed once more alive with the fluttering, preening moths of the twenties.

RIGHT A famous costume: Marie Laurencin's blue velvet suit for the ballet's 'mystery' character

Georgina Parkinson in "LES BICHES"

Svetlana Beriosova as The Hostess

BELOW
Two Little Friends,
dressed in grey (Maryon Lane and Merle Park)

Prancing beach boys: Keith Rosson and Robert Mead

Svetlana Beriosova, as the Hostess desperately striving to avoid boredom, with Keith Rosson and Merle Park

Three Beach Boys inclined to be bores: Keith Rosson, David Blair and Robert Mead

OVERLEAF
Interested spectators: Rosalind Eyre, Elaine Thomas and Virginia Wakelyn watch a liaison— David Blair and Georgina Parkinson

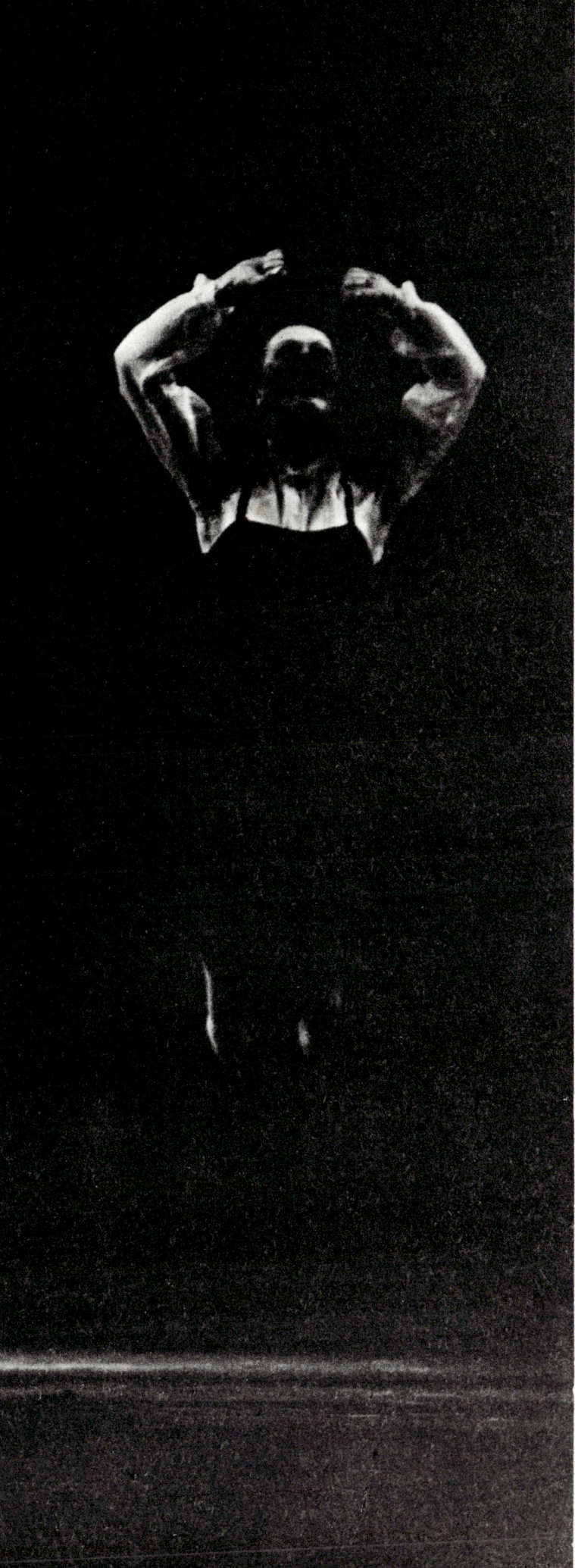

Nijinska's
Les Noces

The second of Nijinska's revivals came as more of a revelatory contrast after the cynical gaiety of *Les Biches*. *Les Noces* sinks its roots deep into the core of Russian peasant life. Its sculptural blocks of choreography shift and change with a bell-like sonority; Nijinska weaving her plain but richly-textured fabric from the same thread of common heritage that Stravinsky also uses in his score. The result is truly a wedding. Two minds open a door for us on a belief and a way of life, though complete comprehension hangs just out of our reach, like an alien sign carved above a door

LEFT   Svetlana Beriosova, utterly simple and utterly perfect as the young bride, pivotal point of the surrounding ritual celebration in *Les Noces*

Beriosova as the bride, with parents (Gerd Larsen and Ray Roberts) and friends

Svetlana Beriosova in LES NOCES

Robert Mead
as the Bridegroom

Corps de ballet patterns in *Les Noces* . . .

... with Georgina Parkinson and Anthony Dowell leading

Bell ringers' hands poised in the final tableau from *Les Noces*

The Sleeping Beauty

A production which helped to launch the Company to international recognition has served its vital purpose for twenty years. Now, a new production of this jewelled classic comes into the repertoire. And the Pepita set-pieces remain to test the classical armoury of successive generations of dancers

Here, as Aurora in Act I, Antoinette Sibley rehearses immediately prior to the Company's 1967 American Tour, where she danced the taxing rôle with conspicuous success

Antoinette Sibley

Antoinette Sibley rehearses with Donald MacLeary as Prince Florimund

45

Sibley and MacLeary rehearse

Merle Park as The Bride in *A Wedding Bouquet* cries of "Charming! charming! charming!"

a deliciously tipsy Josephine in "A Wedding Bouquet"

Frederick Ashton's
A Wedding Bouquet

At the Sadler's Wells Theatre in the Spring of 1937 the curtain went up one evening to reveal for the first time Lord Berners' prim, decorative dropcloth heralding *A Wedding Bouquet,* a ballet inspired by the Gertrude Stein play *They Must Be Wedded to Their Wife*. Berners, whose idea it was for Ashton to use Miss Stein's work as the basis of a ballet (to her subsequent delight) provided the music as well as the décor. The wry, idiosyncratic commentary was spoken then by a chorus, but was ultimately to be replaced more successfully by an orator: Constant Lambert at the 1941 and 1949 revivals, and Robert Helpmann in 1964. It was Helpmann who first played the part of the outrageously raffish Bridegroom in this French provincial wedding, set sometime in the early 1900's. "They all speak as if they expect him to be charming," confides the Orator knowingly. Too true, for the slightly demented Julia (originally one of Fonteyn's earliest solo rôles) who drifts forlornly through the wedding preparations, has already been "ruined" by the cad, and in the ballet's one wistful note, at the end, she finds lonely consolation in the company of her black and tan Mexican terrier Pépé. This apart, all is hilarity; as deft, as seemingly effortless and as palatable as a meringue

Monica Mason in the de Valois rôle of Webster
"Webster was a name that was spoken"

Deanne Bergsma as Josephine, David Drew as Paul and Kenneth Mason as John

Josephine, whom we are told "... may be wearing a gown newly washed and pressed," is excessively devoted to Julia. "Not in any other language could this be written differently," announces Miss Stein flatly. Josephine is also excessively devoted to champagne if the opportunity presents itself. It does. Her ensuing unsteadiness finds ready support from Paul ("Pleasant, vivacious, and quarrelsome") and from John ("An elder brother who regrets the illness of his father")

Violet ("She may be delightful or not, as it happens")
has been pursuing the reluctant Ernest ("May be a victim of himself")
Here, during a diversion, he seeks the opportunity to escape

Vyvyan Lorrayne as Violet, Stanley Holden as Ernest, Ann Jenner as Julia, Margaret Lyons as Pépé, and Leslie Edwards as Arthur

Virginia Wakelyn (Peasant Girl), Alexander Grant (Bridegroom), Rosalind Eyre (Therese)

Merle Park (Bride), David Morse and Dianne Horsham (Peasants)

Rudolf
Nureyev
in

Le

Corsaire

Anthony Dowell as Romeo in Kenneth MacMillan's

Romeo and Juliet

Merle Park
as Juliet, dancing in the Ballroom

BELOW with Derek Rencher as Paris

Merle Park and
Anthony Dowell

Romeo and Juliet

Ashton's
Raymonda pas de deux

Glazunov's lush score for *Raymonda* has been heard in the Royal Ballet repertory on a number of occasions in fragmented form, but it was not used extensively until Rudolf Nureyev reproduced the entire three act ballet for the Company's Touring Section. Both Fonteyn and Wells appeared as the heroine during its initial tour, and have since led the festivities in the truncated version (Act III only) which now remains in the repertory. To jettison so much that is genuinely enjoyable *fin de siècle* seems indulgently extravagant—on a par with the ballet's late 19th century era, in fact. On occasions, Fonteyn still dances in the Ashton interlude from the score, known as *Scène d'Amour,* and even more rarely, Svetlana Beriosova and Donald MacLeary appear in the grand pas de deux which Ashton originally devised for a special gala evening. Here is a reminder of that brilliant showpiece

Margot Fonteyn

in the title role of
Frederick Ashton's
3 Act ballet

Ondine

By turns curious, apprehensive, humourous, grave—the flickering nuances of Fonteyn's unique sprite seem to mirror the dappled sunlight and shadow of her watery domain, as she entwines about her the sweet melancholy of Hans Werner Henze's score

Margot Fonteyn
as Ondine

Margot Fonteyn

Anthony Tudor's *Shadowplay*

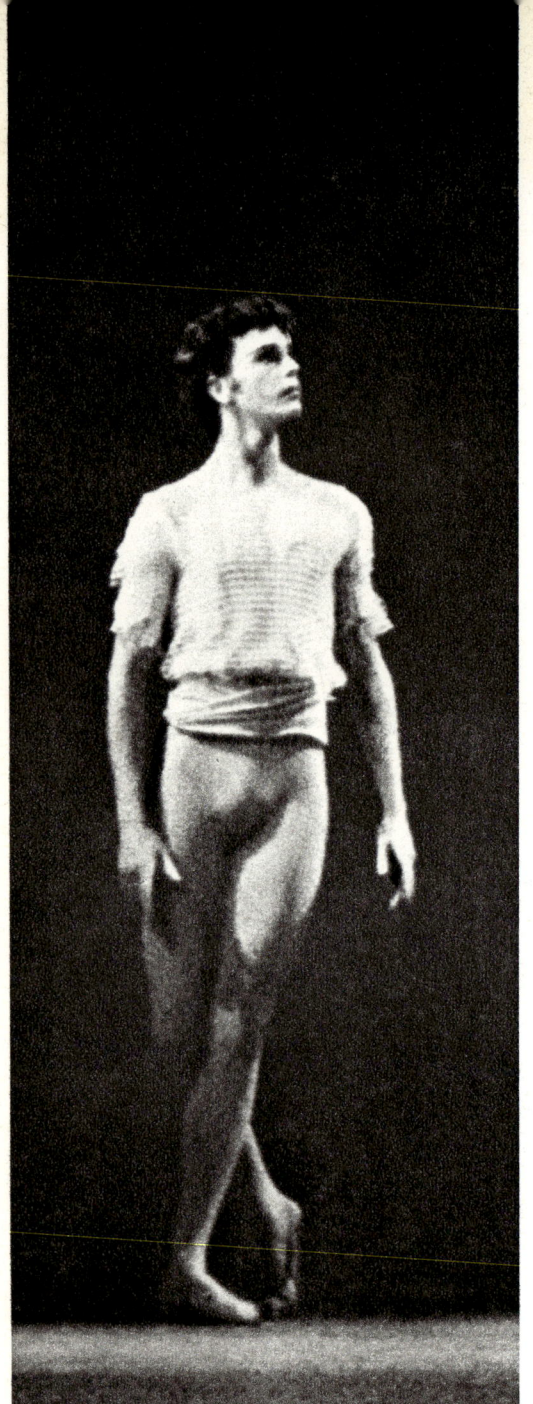

Anthony Dowell
as the
Boy With
Matted Hair

The world of the Boy With Matted Hair lies midway between the jungles of Kipling and of Freud. The Boy seeks a tranquility in which to repose, but in the process of self-discovery is forced to fend off a succession of troubling spirits who seemingly inhabit the penubral domain in which he finds himself. His equilibrium is successively threatened by ape-like Arboreals who mock his efforts at composure, and by both male and female spirits, the Terrestial and the Celestial, who reflect the desires hidden within himself.

Kipling's *The Jungle Book* provided the French composer Koechlin with the basic inspiration for his score *Les Bandar-Log* (1939), which Tudor uses to such advantage in this strangely fascinating work. His casting was flawless, with fine opportunities provided for Anthony Dowell—the fluent, oiled-silk technique and youthful grace here complemented by the sure projection of a mind troubled by the confusing outlines of the world around him. Miss Park's cool authority as the bitch-goddess Celestial made her pas de deux with with The Boy a particularly haunting highlight of the ballet, which in its entirety displays a master choreographer in full command of his resources

Disturbing encounter with the Terrestial (Derek Rencher)

pas de deux after the airborne
arrival (PRECEDING PAGE)
Merle Park as
the Celestial

The duality in the nature of the Celestial reveals itself in a remorseless attack directed against the boy

In a mountingly frenzied attack, the forces of the Celestial and the Terrestial combine in a 'paper tiger' which harrasses The Boy. In desperation, he finally faces the monster and hurls himself into its jaws

Having freed himself from the grip of his tormentors, The Boy's dive disperses the monster's form. He explodes free and the Terrestial is now powerless to contain him. An Arboreal watches with a newly respectful awe

Seated once more at the base of the great tree, The Boy finds a new calmness apparent. In ordered pattern, the Arboreals turn towards their superior Master

Donald MacLeary rehearses *Apollo*

George Balanchine's
Apollo *in rehearsal*

This early classic in Balanchine's career was first performed under the title *Apollon Musagète*, in Paris on June 12th 1928. Together with Stravinsky's score, the work and the way it was performed—by Serge Lifar, with Tchernicheva, Dubrovska, and Nikitina—was hailed as a resounding triumph.

Revivals have been numerous; the present one by the Royal Ballet was painstakingly supervised—perhaps too much so. Like hygenically sealed food, the contents were clear and apparently appetising, yet they proved to be strangely lacking in the authentic flavour when finally sampled. Even the most robust ballets can prove waywardly delicate under transplanted conditions; time alone will tell whether this one can put out fresh roots and bloom again

Svetlana Beriosova as Terpsichore, with Donald MacLeary as Apollo

Beriosova and MacLeary

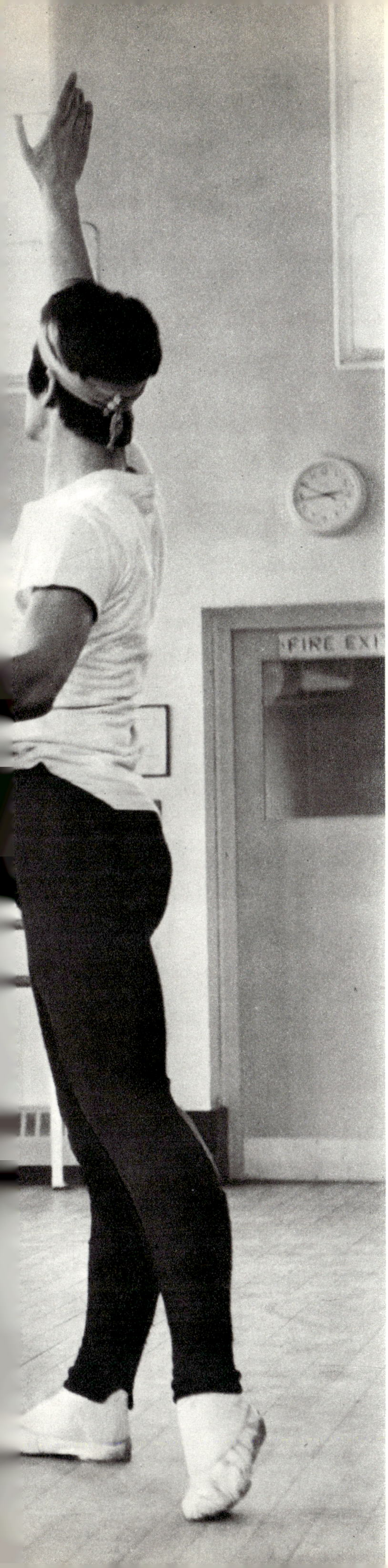

Polyhymnia: Monica Mason

Calliope: Georgina Parkinson

Terpsichore: Svetlana Beriosova

Beneath the Temple of Bacchus, Baalbek,
Margot Fonteyn and Rudolf Nureyev rehearse

The Royal Ballet on Tour

Both sections of the Royal Ballet undertake extensive tours abroad; the independent Touring Section spends the bulk of its time on the move, while the rather larger 'home' section undertakes the frequent and taxing North American tours, and other selective excursions, such as the Eastern European Tour of 1966. The spectacular setting provided by the Baalbek Festival in the Lebanon must be unique for its combination of romanticism and grandeur

RIGHT
Deirdre O'Conaire by the resin box on the temporary stage at Baalbek. In the background, Michael Coleman and David Wall try pirouettes on the raked stage

Raymonda rehearsal on stage in the Teatro Nuova, Spoleto. Watching with Sir Frederick Ashton are John Field and Henry Legerton

Rudolf Nureyev
in the title rôle
of Robert Helpmann's

Hamlet

during performance
at Baalbek

Nureyev as Hamlet

Rehearsing the rôle (below) with Johar Mosaval as the Gravedigger. Margot Fonteyn (Ophelia) watches from the wings area

RIGH[T]
Doreen Wells in Nichola[s] Georgiadis' costume for th[e] central character [of] MacMillan's *Danse Concertante*

Danses Concertantes

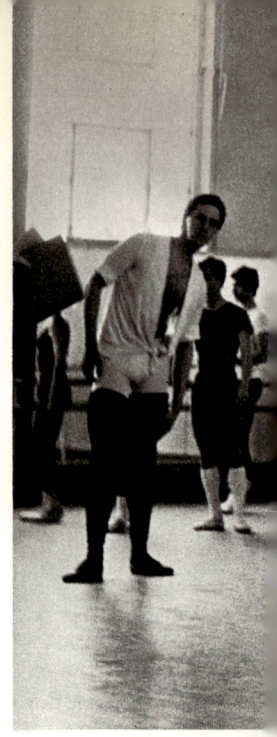

Kenneth MacMillan's astonishingly accomplished first ballet (1955) maintains its place in the repertory; the deft and quirky imagery is a happy foil to these same elements in Stravinsky's score

During a *Danses Concertantes* rehearsal, Adrian Grater leans in agonized sympathy as Paul Clarke and Alfreda Thorogood sort out a tricky jump and catch

Paul Clarke, as one of the ballet's characters in a moment of temporary repose, showing the spiky finger-element present throughout this ballet

Brenda Last's sparkling and exhuberant technique finds numerous outlets—from the pert humour of *Danses Concertantes,* to the fun-loving heroine of Ashton's *La Fille Mal Gardée* and the female acrobat in *The Invitation*

Kenneth MacMillan's *The Invitation*

Shirley Grahame as The Wife,
rehearsing with Graham Powell as The Boy

Patricia Ruanne
with Hendrik Davel

The drama of MacMillan's popular ballet lies in the tangled emotions of young love, the innocence blighted by the intervention of adult passions

Patricia Ruanne is seen rehearsing here as the girl in the story—on the left, with her cousin and prankish young friends; and responding naïvely to the subtle partnership of The Husband (Adrian Grater)
BELOW AND OVERLEAF

Artistic exasperation at a model's teasing
interruptions, in Ashton's popular bohemian Romance

Frederick Ashton's
The Two Pigeons

David Wall as the young painter and Doreen Wells as his restless model friend

Doreen Wells and David Wall

trouble over the possession of a chair
leads to temporary estrangement

127

The fun continues with the artist apparently now resigned to his lot

The arrival of gypsies in the studio revives the artist's spirits. Here, he flirts with the Gypsy Girl (Elizabeth Anderton) who is encouraged by her friends

The artist's obvious switch in attentions begins to worry his girl-friend and erstwhile model

Flashing temperament and feminine rivalries now lead to trouble

Pepio, the artist, is thoroughly captivated by the gypsy girl. Her gypsy lover (Richard Farley) broods on the situation. Later, when Pepio decides to follow the interloper, Gourouli fears she may now have lost Pepio for ever

All is not lost. Abandoned by the gypsies after a fight, Pepio returns to the studio a chastened young man. He has brought with him the pigeon which Gourouli had sent to look for him

They commence the ballet's concluding ecstatic pas de deux

Pigeons re-united—
the final moment
of the ballet

Swan Lake

Presumably the most enduring and the most frequently mauled ballet of all time. The Royal Ballet has done more than most to preserve intact the authentic Pepita and Ivanov sections in so far as they are still known; one half of the Company retaining the 'original' version from Sadler's Wells days, the other half experimenting with new productions and interpolated passages. They have still to find the golden solution. Meanwhile the quest continues and yet another new production seems due for launching on those moonlit waters

Svetlana Beriosova, one of this generation's great Swan Queens, rehearses the lakeside scenes with Donald MacLeary as Prince Siegfried

Jane Landon
with Nicholas
Benton

Grahame
and
Beaumont

Shirley Grahame and Piers Beaumont

Doreen Wells and David Wall rehearse the Ballroom Act

Doreen Wells and David Wall

Shirley Grahame rehearses as Odile in the Ballroom scene

David Wall rehearses Prince Siegfried's variation from the Ballroom scene

David Wall

John Field rehearses two of his gifted protegées—
Doreen Wells and David Wall

Director of the section of the Royal Ballet known as the Touring Company, John Field has earned unstinted praise for his efforts in bringing on young and inexperienced dancers while maintaining an overall company standard under what are often the most exhausting and frustrating of conditions. His work is rewarded when talents blossom to star status away from 'home' and return to The Royal Opera House to be welcomed as major attractions. Field, together with Henry Legerton, produce between them a company which gives performances in the truest sense of the word

Frederick Ashton's

The Dream

Antoinette Sibley in the rôle of Titania in Ashton's delicate and evocative masterpiece originally produced for the Shakespeare Quatercentenary in 1964

Alexander Grant
as Bottom—
transfigured
and
released

Antoinette Sibley
as Titania
with
Alexander Grant
as Bottom

Anthony Dowell in his rôle as Oberon
dances the pas de deux with Antoinette Sibley

Differences resolved—Titania and Oberon at the conclusion of the ballet

Ronald Emblen as Bottom

Second production of THE DREAM

Keith Martin as Puck

Merle Park as Titania

Merle Park . . . with Stanley Holden as Bottom

Misty confusion reigns as Puck works his magic amidst the quartet of lovers

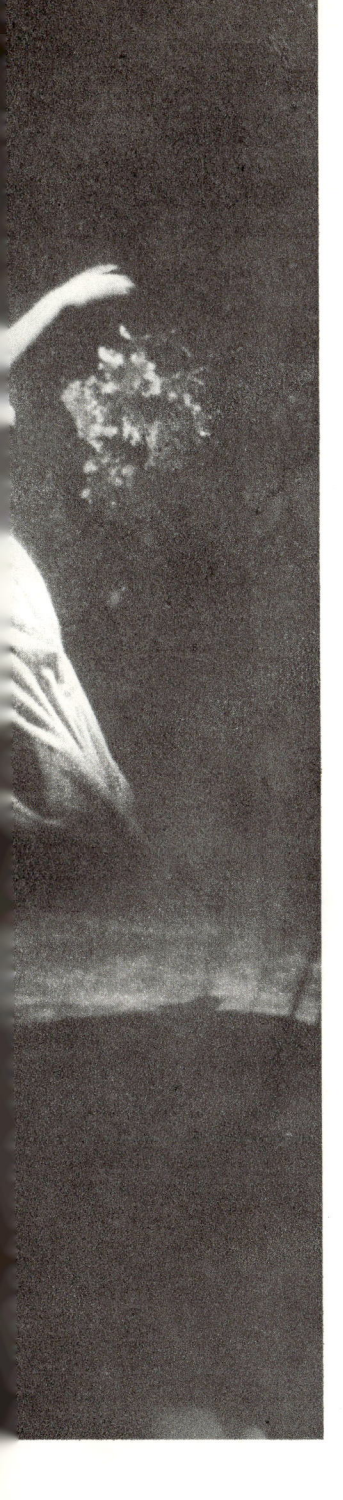

BELOW   More of Puck's handiwork, as Titania (Merle Park) is enraptured by the company of the transformed Bottom (Stanley Holden)

Lucette Aldous
as Titania
with
David Wall
as Oberon

Kenneth MacMillan's
Concerto

danced to the breezy Second Piano Concerto of Shostakovitch

ABOVE Elizabeth Anderton and David Wall

Doreen Wells and Richard Farley in the elegiac section

ABOVE David Wall

LEFT Wells and Farley

Jane Landon in the third movement of *Concerto*

Georgina Parkinson and Desmond Doyle in MacMillan's *Images of Love* (1964)

Song of the Earth

Belatedly acquired from John Cranko's Stuttgart company which gained the ballet's initial creation after previous rebuffs from a timid Covent Garden, *Song of the Earth* was acclaimed as Kenneth MacMillan's finest work to date—a ballet of profound beauty and power from a choreographer who has already given Ballet a host of fascinating and vital creations.

MacMillan's choreography in *Song of the Earth* seems a cool and inspired synthesis of the previous ten years' outpourings, but perhaps more than any other one work, the wayward, uneven, but often inspired moments of 1964's *Images of Love* (see preceding page) can be seen in retrospect to herald the later ballet's new range in depth in expressiveness. Like all of MacMillan's work, it is deeply classical in spirit, eschewing any more than the merest hints of a chinoiserie that might have over-embroidered this work—had the choreographer been too obsessed with the fact that it was Chinese poems which inspired Mahler.

There are those who put forward the hypothesis that it is invalid to use Mahler's work as the foundation of a ballet, on the basis that the musical masterpiece is so complete as to preclude any additional distraction; that one creation must inevitably suffer at the expense of the other. The fact remains that MacMillan has created an infinitely beautiful work, and that work has arisen heart and soul out of Gustav Mahler's own masterpiece. One artistic creation has given birth to another, and Mahler himself might have found comfort in that thought

LEFT
Anthony Dowell as the masked Messenger of Death, the benign omnipresence who overshadows the entire ballet

Georgina Parkinson

Vyvyan Lorrayne

Jennifer Penney
in the Third Song

OVERLEAF

Third Song: About Youth

Jennifer Penney
with
Keith Martin
Frank Freeman
Michael Coleman
Lambert Cox

Rosalind Eyre   Dianne Horsham

Fourth Song: About Beauty

"Young girls are picking flowers
Picking lotus buds on the river bank"

Ann Jenner   Carole Hill

LEFT AND RIGHT
Georgina Parkinson
and Kenneth Mason

204

ABOVE
Georgina Parkinson
and David Drew

LEFT Vyvyan Lorrayne and David Gayle

Ann Jenner

Vyvyan Lorrayne

Ann Jenner

Jennifer Penney

Monica Mason
in the central rôle

h Vyvyan Lorrayne
Jennifer Penney

Monica Mason
and
Anthony Dowell

Monica Mason with Donald MacLeary and Anthony Dowell

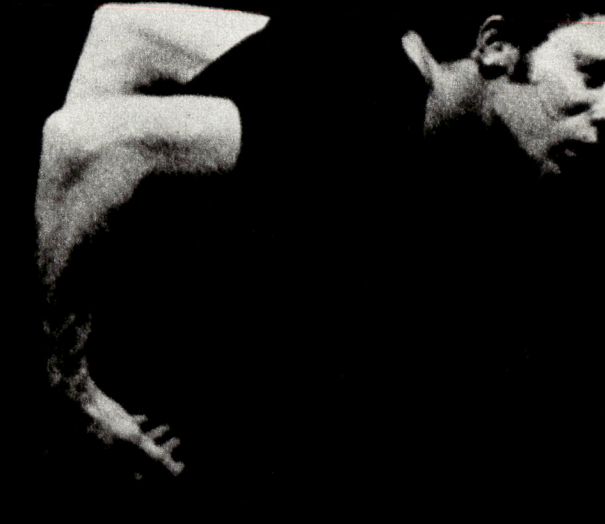

Dowell, Mason and MacLeary

Sixth Song: The Farewell
Monica Mason
and Donald MacLeary

Frederick Ashton's
Sinfonietta

The vast output of Britain's greatest choreographer has been as complete and as varied as a spectrum; it has ranged from baroque magnificence to the most delicate etching. The moods and nuances are infinite, the musical felicities inviolate. One of Ashton's more rarely used colours in that personal spectrum is the cool, blue strata of air and space. When Ashton does venture into this area, his dancers throw off the limitations of an earthly environment. Bathed in moon pallor they become stellar constellations. Turned, floated, revolved, entwined, they maintain the weightlessness of a human spacecraft forming eternal convolutions in space. *Monotones* was a recent excursion by Ashton into this abstract arena; *Sinfonietta's* Second Movement continues this aerial exploration on a larger scale

LEFT
Doreen Wells and David Wall in one of Ashton's intricate patterns—arrived at with seeming simplicity and unbroken ease

RIGH
Wells airborne in th
second movement
Sinfoniet
(Music by Malcol
Williamso

Lucette Aldous, as the female 'stellar body', is supported during a rehearsal of the second movement from *Sinfonietta*

The movement as costumed. Doreen Wells in rotation here

Doreen Wells
with the
five
supporting
cavaliers

David Wall airborne this time,
in a swirling manège from the last movement of *Sinfoni*

Michael Somes rehearses Antoinette Sibley and Anthony Dowell for their debut in Cinderella

Antoinette Sibley and Anthony Dowell

Michael Somes preparing the pair for their first appearance in the ballet—on the second night of the 1967 New York season

Michael Somes
rehearses
Antoinette Sibley

Antoinette Sibley and Anthony Dowell

Frederick Ashton's
Cinderella

Frederick Ashton's choice for his first full length ballet, mounted in December 1948, was Prokofiev's *Cinderella*. The title rôle was designed for Margot Fonteyn, although she was subsequently prevented by injury from appearing in the first performance of the ballet. Ashton borrowed from English pantomime tradition for his Christmas ballet, having the rôles of the Ugly Sisters played *en travesti*—both he and Robert Helpmann mining such a wealth of comedy and characterful by-play from the rôles that they seem to claim the lion's share of the action; Ashton's shy, fussy Sister, a bundle of thwarted longings constantly at the mercy of Helpmann's blush-making virago.

In countries less familiar with English 'panto dame' tradition, the playing of the sisters by men has made audiences a little uncertain in their reactions, more so when they find the heroine deployed for long periods in motionless contemplation on the sidelines. Critics have long expressed the hope that Sir Frederick might revise the plainer ensemble passages of this ballet to match the sparkle and tenderness of its best sections, which are glorious. These hopes have not materialized, but it does mean that, historically, the Royal Ballet displays untouched the first three-act ballet by its master choreographer. As such its interest will presumably increase with the years.

And nothing will dim the memory of Fonteyn's heart-touching Cinderella. Ravishingly beautiful in her dull rags, demure and graceful in her ballroom finery, Fonteyn welds her rôle into a portrait study that leaves no facet of the character unlit, her joys and her sorrows become the audiences' vital concern, and never can sweeter performances have been entrusted to them

LEFT
Margot Fonteyn
as
Cinderella

Sisterly squabble:
Sir Frederick Ashton
and Sir Robert Helpmann
as Cinderella's step-sisters
with Leslie Edwards in the
rôle of the father

With the remnant of the sisters' shawl, Cinderella devises her own amusement in the empty kitchen

Helpmann
and
Ashton

Cinderella (Fonteyn) has been goaded into a defiant interruption of the step-sisters' bullying tactics employed against their long-suffering father. Almost immediately, a strange and awesome light begins to fill the darkening kitchen

The eerie light has heralded the arrival of the Fairy Godmother. Later revealed in her true splendour (BELOW) she promises Cinderella that the pumpkin shall be transformed into a golden coach. At the end of Act I, Cinderella is indeed swept off to the Prince's Ball, disappearing into the mist as the curtains fall

Fragile as porcelain, with her starry train shimmering in the candlelight, Cinderella advances into the ballroom. She moves forward as in a trance, watched by the awestruck Jester (Alexander Grant) acting as train-bearer

Ballroom Escorts— LEFT

Wayne Sleep's 'Napoleon' maintains dignity under trying conditions...

BELOW
... while Derek Rencher's 'Wellington' copes similarly with the other sister

Margot Fonteyn as Cinderella

Donald MacLeary as her prince

The step-sisters fail to recognize Cinderella in her new glory. Secure in this knowledge, Cinderella hands one of them the largest of three costly and rare oranges

She soon loses it to the conniving and forceful sister, gaining in exchange the smallest orange

RIGHT
After their hilarious exit, Cinderella enters the deserted ballroom, seeking the Prince

In the ballroom, Cinderella dances a
grand pas de deux, alone with the dazzled Prince.
(David Blair as the Prince, with Margot Fonteyn as Cinderella)

RIGHT
Fonteyn
and Blair

Back home, and momentary triumph as one of the sisters
imagines that she has successfully fitted her own
gross foot into the frail slipper, found by the
Prince after Cinderella's precipitate midnight
departure from the Ball. The sister's first step
is about to disillusion her, to the open amusement of
the attendants
(Robert Helpmann, with Douglas Steuart and David Morse)

True love revealed. David Blair as the Prince discovering Cinderella (Fonteyn) to be the rightful owner of the slipper

Cinderella and her Prince united